Ellie-Sue Doesn't Want to Play

Written by

Catherine Wilkinson

DEDICATION

Dedicated to my lovely
little friend Elle.

The series of emotional awareness books are designed to be interesting for your child. I hope that they will find it interesting to learn about the different emotions and things that they can see in their world. With the different books and also the SELIA Kids program, my aim is to promote an introduction to emotional, cognitive and environmental awareness. Research has shown that a foundation in awareness can lead to better choices, decision making and problem solving. And that these can lead to a more fulfilling life for the individual and the people around them. Part of the importance of learning these skills is the practice of slowing down to become aware of and acknowledge what is happening around us.

Often so much is happening in our lives and our children's lives that children can get over stimulated and overly involved in the situation without realising. The danger in this is that behaviours can happen that are not healthy, or sometimes not how we would usually have liked to have behaved ourselves or have had our children behave. When we become over stimulated and bombarded with information, be it social, environmental, relational, or emotional, we start to lose the opportunity to think clearly and make decisions.

Critically we lose the opportunity to learn the skills we need to live healthy and fulfilling lives. Often we don't realise we do not have the right skills to use within the challenging situation until we really need them! This is exactly what these series of books are designed to do, to teach your child and open the communication lines to develop strong social and emotional skills. Skills such as resilience, confidence, teamwork, leadership, self discipline, delayed gratification, and emotional regulation.

You will find as you spend time with your child with the different books, and implementing the techniques, that your relationship with your child will change. You will notice your own understanding is improved, your child is more responsive, and your relationship will be strengthened. The questions within the books are designed to promote conversation in general, but also to set a precedent of your child feeling comfortable in talking with you about their feelings from a very early stage where your relationship is the most important one in their life. Please use the questions as a prompt, though expand and add your own experiences to connect with your child where possible. I hope that you will enjoy them too!

As you read through, the storyline is followed by the large circle on the page. The questions to ask your child or for you to help them ponder are followed by the small circle on the page. Please use these as a guide, but add in your own experience or questions wherever you feel the need. This will help make the story and the communication relevant for you and your child, and also allows for a greater understanding and learning experience.

Catherine Wilkinson

BA (Psych)(Hons), Dip Prof Couns, Cert Frontline Management, Cert 1 Trainer, ...and Mum!

Aston and Elle are great friends. They love to spend time together playing.

How do you think they are feeling? How can you tell?

Usually, when they see each other, they share a big hello hug. They giggle, and hug, and squeeze, and laugh.

Look at them having a squeezy hug! Do you like to have hugs?

Today when they met, Elle didn't want a big hello hug.

What do you think is happening?

Aston looked at Elle and wondered why she did not want to play.

Why do you think Elle doesn't want to play? brainstorm a few possibilities.

He could
see her eyes
were a little closed
and teary, with her
eyebrows a little
raised in the
middle.

Point to them.

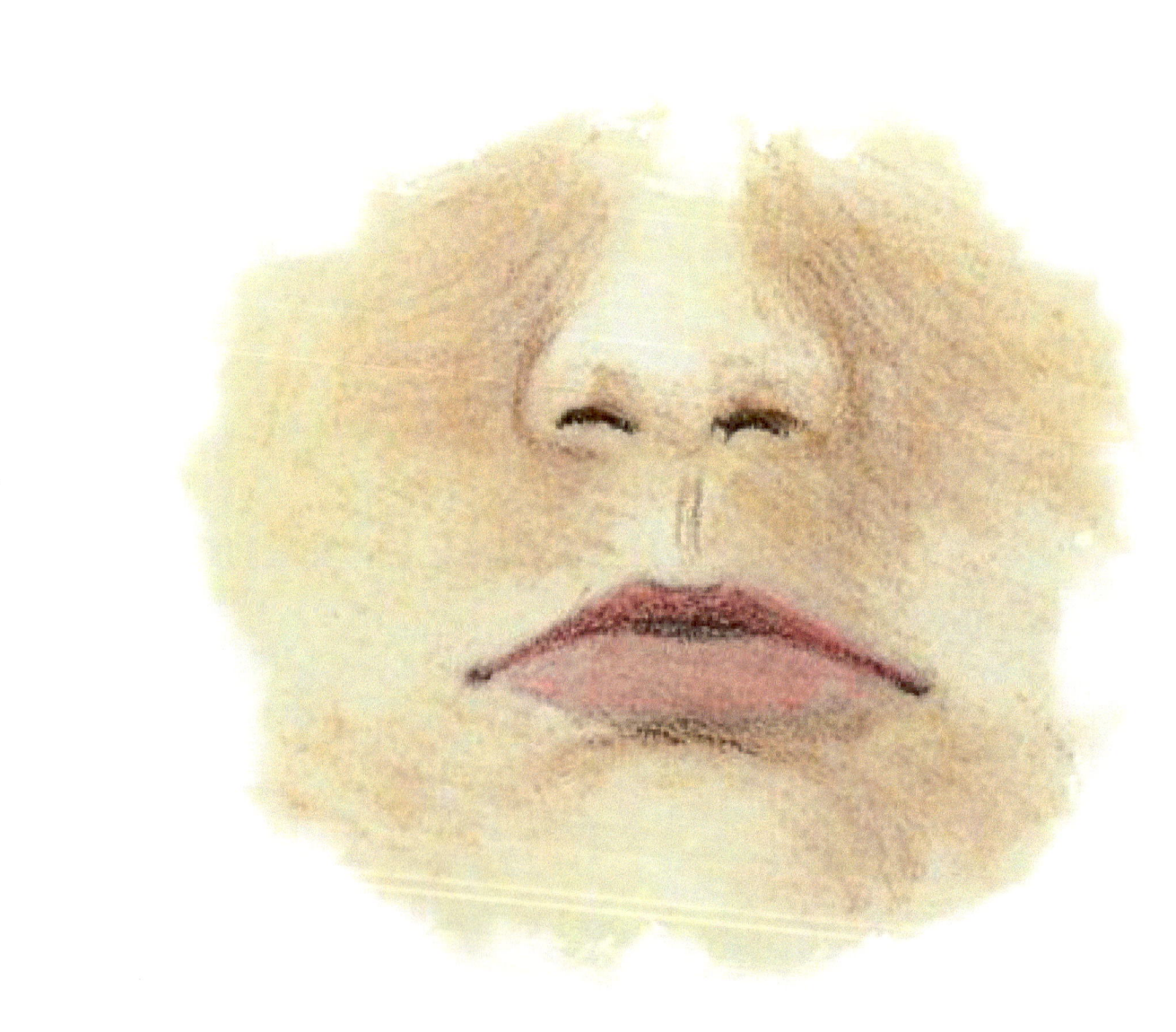

He could see her bottom lip was poking out and her mouth was rounded down, like a frown.

Point to them.

And Aston could see she was standing all alone just looking down at the floor.

How do you think Elle is feeling? How can you tell?

He thought to himself, "Elle looks Sad."

Do you remember a time when you felt sad? What happened? How did you feel happy again?

"I know what I can do," Aston thought. He went and gave Elle his favorite cuddle blanket to comfort her.

What are some other ways Aston could show Elle that he cared? Brainstorm a few...

Elle felt happy to know that Aston cared about her.

Who are some people you care about? Who are some people who care about you? Brainstorm some. Include police, teachers, etc.

SELIA KIDS PROGRAM

SELIA Kids is a division of the Social and Emotional Learning Institute Australia (SELIA). It is an opportunity for parents and carers to connect with their children and teach them the vital skills they need whilst growing in these critical stages of development and especially towards starting school. Skills for development that they will carry through into adolescence and adulthood.

The Social and Emotional Learning Institute Australia (SELIA) was founded to establish social and emotional learning (SEL) as a fundamental part of child education. We operate a multi faceted approach working with families with children from 0 to 6 years through our **SELIA Kids** program, and working with principals and leaders from primary schools throughout Australia. Our consultants and program developers work with advisors in the United States, the UK and New Zealand to ensure up to date and established SEL practices.

SELIA is *Putting the Pieces Together* for child academic, social, and emotional education.

Social and emotional learning (SEL) is a strategy for developing the essential life skills necessary for greater success throughout all the different aspects of life. SEL builds the skills we all need to manage our lives, our relationships, and our study or work, more effectively and with greater satisfaction. Skills such as recognising and managing our emotions, making responsible decisions, handling challenging situations constructively, and establishing fulfilling relationships.

In respect of children, these skills help them to understand what they are feeling and make appropriate behaviour response choices that further help them to keep themselves safe and resolve conflicts or confrontations more effectively.

The Collaborative for Social and Emotional Learning (CASEL) has identified five core groups of social and emotional competencies:

· *Self-awareness*—accurately assessing one's feelings, interests, values, and strengths; maintaining a well-grounded sense of self-confidence

· *Self-management*—regulating one's emotions to handle stress, control impulses, and persevere in overcoming obstacles; setting and monitoring progress toward personal and academic goals; expressing emotions appropriately

· *Social awareness*—being able to take the perspective of and empathize with others; recognizing and appreciating individual and group similarities and differences; recognizing and using family, school, and community resources

· *Relationship skills*—establishing and maintaining healthy and rewarding relationships based on cooperation; resisting inappropriate social pressure; preventing, managing, and resolving interpersonal conflict; seeking help when needed

· *Responsible decision-making*—making decisions based on consideration of ethical standards, safety concerns, appropriate social norms, respect for others, and likely consequences of various actions; applying decision-making skills to academic and social situations; contributing to the well-being of one's school and community

Please visit our website at www.seliakids.com.au

or for primary school educators www.selinstituteaustralia.com.au

All Titles in the Series: